Among the Names

Among the Names

—

Maxine Chernoff

Apogee Press
Berkeley · California
2005

Acknowledgements

The author wishes to thank the editors of the following magazines
for originally publishing poems in this manuscript: *Denver Quarterly,
Hambone, Smartish Pace, Slope, New American Writing, Five Fingers Review,
Minnesota Review, nth position* [England], *26, Parnassus West, Luna,
His Bibitur, Small Town, jacket* [Australia], and *14 Hills.*

Book design by Philip Krayna Design, Berkeley, California.

Cover sculpture, *20 Jahre Einsamkeit* by Anselm Kiefer, printed with the
permission of the Kunstmuseum Wolfsburg. Photo by Helge Mundt.

ISBN 0-9744687-8-9. Library of Congress Catalog Card Number 2004117970.

Published by Apogee Press, Post Office Box 8177, Berkeley CA, 94707-8177.
www.apogeepress.com

as ever, for Paul

Table of Contents

Among the Names

[flux: isolation]

        permission for sympathy
in the "chemistry of man"
            (O spirit
O home)
         And yet new dicta

      seek experience

by degrees
   of strangeness
       "the unlettered boy"
            knew virtue as humor

        in remarkable increase
"throat opened"
          will abandoned to

a hieroglyphic

     of   undivided   light

[the world owes the world more than the world can pay]

a ray
       like music:
"pertinence
       and beauty everyday"
              many parts rejoice:
flower leaves, paint boxes,
           coral and lambs
       generosity in fate
       but rich men and kings
who receive a gift poorly
           fear favor or blackmail
       glut (then loss)

       If gifts might speak:
  "you do not need me"

    like a goldsmith
or loved one

          finding rectitude
(a way to love)
in interference

[*present/poison*]

To choose
    from among them
a suitable root:
      "to bestow venom"
         links forever
   "I give you this"/"and this
     in return"
binds us in pouring

        the potable bond
yet fearing
      our neighbors
(as ourselves)
   we hope
 for a charm

     (to live &
        be well)
    drinking
displeasure's   impossible

      fruit

[da/a-da]

to take and

receive
   in language
and space
   a calling
of ancients
a root of gratitude
   the ripe
   ears of grain
   ("her snazzy
            new Lexus")
so suitors invite
            the sale of guests
the anger of gods
      returns as destruction
at the sacred banquet
the feast   the damage
   the shapely urn:
            each thing we build
we also break

[mana/machine]

"The disability

   of all
  finite thought"
extricates

        a limitless series
           of misunderstandings

(Do dogs misunderstand / or
are they

too honest?)
      Argonauts of emotion,

magic, and mystification,

      are we not speaking
in rustic Portuguese
         when inquiry veers
to life-blood
and categories?
         Let us discuss
    the dead
moon's halo
        in morphemes and
phonemes
     I'll give

  the signal

    to problematize

[In giving you I give myself.]

A worthy object
        bond of souls
which given

results

        in exchange of
hau   but failing
to reciprocate—
a religious concept
            misunderstood—
  will wound
                one   deeply   and
            then perhaps
vengeance
of god or man
        depending on
what
    quits the body
        at death—

soul   or capital—

  as if a shadow
or cape to give
        someone
whose shoulders
need convincing

[things are confounded with the spirits who made them]

To dig
       for an object

            (ultimate in character)
"multiplicity
in motion"

         total reciprocity
yes   there is contrast
between festival & war
           as with enchantment
of "monstrous products"
(would bombs fit here?)
  (our gift to history)
        "the tribes"
"the sea journeys"
       "the precious things"
a wheel of provisions
     topped by
a walrus head
as certain corporations
  Maypole profits
     to men in ties &
Western philosophy
       or Japanese exchange

of perfect boxes
     the sun too
implicated
    in circularity

[not having known how to give]

The Sun King
      takes
(as is his job)
      or rather
is given
      Madame's attention
the circle
      of time and of
the gift
partition of
   law and economy
"I give you my now"
      precludes the antithesis
(& here the vulgar
circle again)
Can we see instead
perhaps an arrow
      of one's desire
aimed at intention?
     to bestow
   as ruse   (no calculation)
results in secret
economy
"across the forgetting/the non-keeping"
     I did not know
(the gun was loaded)
     I did not know
it was a gift

[translucent mold of me it shall be you]

"translating"
      "the roofs
of mouths"
("she saw them
and loved them")
         "beards"   "glistened"
      "and yet you stand" "the sustenance"
          "and accretion"
"forbidden voices"

        "clarified"
"divine"   "the hands"   "the songs"
       "O Death"
     "bequeath" "the little light"
"the hearing
of others"
       "solemn" "note"
       "of tongues"
    "the gift"   "below"

[to bear a gift for mortals]

"shape did move"
  "a shadow across me"
"upon the page"
  "introspection"
  "& eyes" ("the world's ornament")
  "on the green"
"a white boy goes"
  "the specter"
"subscribes"
    "to speechless tribes"
  "etcetera"
 "it flows"
   "& nature remains"
"its soiled green feet"
  "he turned
into a tree"
"to form a link"
    "with art"

  "who giveth
  "the future" ("essential unity")

   "of eye and hand"
    "who giveth"

"first fruits" & "the young bride"

"when I"
"a correspondent"
"take such additions"

[delights to endure all things]

not charity
    the giving
Dear Cedric
       thundercloud   resonance
of all spiritual
     those who are
children
illuminating
        thought
& lights
    of the inner folds
no words
     or deeds over
  Half Dome
     let loose
nothing finer
    than those
myriad mirrors
     flashing
the tragic

       the seeking
of desire   (the charity)
    of art & wish

[mine/not mine]

that history is
        phallocentric
the "cuntditionality" of
        masculine
            desire   the wanting
              the conserving
from the beginning
           over the abyss
goes
          all possible difference
but having/
          not having
in crystallization
        (femininity repressed)
           the non-inclusion
(it wears you out)
            mynosemybodymyskinmytongue
all things
female
      do not
hold
overflow

in knowledge
control   confinement

in everything
   the mother
the maker lover of things
   never measures
     or counts
  what she gives
in giving
    takes back
otherness
takes back
herself whole

[fall back into the anarchy]

"a deep polygamous tendency"

> infrastructure
> > of brides
(why not give men?)
heterosexuality
> > a smoothing of love
of self
> among men
who find in the taking
> the gift they seek
(use = accumulation)
> & so he gathers
women
> labor
cars & ice
> he does not know
how her
value escapes—
> ("hole
in the symbolic")
or why

the ice

machine

                labors on
in the night
  ("breach in discourse")
sharing the cult
            of the mirror   he's
"lamb of God"
            (his master)
            sexual
pleasure   appropriation
            of wealth
debt
credit
            by degrees
of desire
            & she too forfeits
in taking
the name
        in giving herself
to the abstract
value

[when a happy thing falls]

"between world and toy"
        "his widowed skin"
"leapt over"
           "in that womb"
"someone else"
      "in the middle
of fate"
"you hold each other"
        "what's your proof?"
      "its clutching"   "upturned"
"their whole eyes"

"coins copulating"
      (in that economy
      of shadows)
"a pure event"
    "blooms"
"without symbol"

[that time gives it its form]

       never barley
(symbol of frailty)
       money or eggs
hazardous to
       the holy man
a reply / a riposte
       a dishonor
to steal a mule
       by treachery
in sleep
for example
       discrete moves
in boxing or chess
       (the rule as obstacle)
overeagerness
       ingratitude too
or misrecognition
so many errors
create suspense
& by illusion
       a world is
built
       and collapses

[and in the background the origin of aqueducts]

you giver
      interrupting
the barely needed
      the boast of ships
        coupling
    to forget
how far   the whole
    rescues your
blooming
      your destructible

    "breath-stops"
      which capture

a younger god
      whose goal
is a hybrid
of mirror
    and you

[both deceiving and deceived]

"an open secret"
transcends
honor
        (murder in
a purse of coins
        thrown out the window
of state
and church)
yet generosity   can be
learned
        & in so doing
conscience itself
        is destiny
suspicion results
        from misrecognition
am I myself
in giving myself
        in calculation
violence secures
symbolic power
exchange & deception
        counterfeit
the illusion
finding itself
tenacious
    cedes its power
to
        universal
        forms of
respect

[the list of fatalities includes the book]

discourse = the language
of bees
            (the book reduced
to paper
and pulp)
"posthistorical dandies" (madman & lover)

give profusely

        the State (self-conscious)

                gives away
                    its nothing-
                            ness
                an empty vessel
                    slips on a verandah
    "economy as mysticism"
                    the future "cruel"
            beyond the fence
                of the present
    see how the edge
            slips over the edge

[to give without falling prey]

       even in refusal
a gift is destroyed
(history as amnesia)
to minimize betrayal
seek ingratitude
(says the seer)
"I give you a world
       and emptied
I return it
       a seeker of emptiness
my without is
       not hidden
but beyond
       being
       beyond myself

and my fetters"
the gift is not
   alms or begging
       counterfeit or debt
orgiastic mysteries

replaced

by the null set

       the nothing

        the liturgies
of ambiguity
        the magnanimity
of blind refusal

[in praise of uselessness]

to name
the unnameable

(sprach Zarathustra)
                    "you great star"
  you who
give anything
      of love
          "though the artist withholds"
                  & the wise man
  has no
  personal friends
(his presence angelic
          his face
  honey)
          so Zarathustra
tosses the ball
which is nothing
which is
values
& transvaluation
          you, prophet,
  squandering wealth

"with a thousand hands"

          becoming a robber

in "bestowing love"
        you give
that which you are
            in owning
yourself
becoming
        another
            owning nothing

[a dollar love]

his death
   would be
the first future
      to break   (gently)
         when it came

(confidence based
      on a rate of exchange)

& love's
     poor stowaway
innocent
         or calculated—
(marriage and children
     Reno and divorce)
  compared to
the love
     that knows
no future—
hollow
     emptied
spare in its vows
    which,

without language
speaks
of not holding

[to bully the gods, we ask their blessings]

the hedge-priest bandies
terms and conditions
  "I'll scratch your back"

      etc.
as when in Italy
     she seeks
to gain
health
by punching
a saint
repeatedly
demonology too
requires such
      motives
as seen on TV
the afternoon type
          the square-jawed man
rendezvous with the woman
    in the tawdry café
where actors are seen
     but back to Egypt where

gods were bullied
     out of their tombs
into legend and myth
     then onto prayer
a humble petition
suggesting our reverence
for what
     we can't own

[a flow of speech]

I give you a word
        its gift
to be measured,
        dear listener,
who wants
the object
and thing
        in common language
whose value explodes
        as we meta-
communicate
        God into flesh
of thought
        or voice
(an organ of   breath)
        the life you
save   may   be
        non-
linguistic
succeeding
        though words
give way

        as in

the dream
when sheaves are
        counted
moon and stars bow

down to the boy
              who names
the objects nature
              bestows
who counts himself
              among the names

[perfectslave to:]

"submission
          is a choice
I make"

          *

"I consider
          my submission
a gift   that can
          only be given
from the heart"

          *

          "a gift you give
without expectation
          of return"

          *

"keep your gifts
          my missy
came to me
          needing to
          be owned
          because she has
     desires
          wants
& needs
that   only   I
can
          satisfy"

*

"it can't be given
        or taken
back
it's a commitment"

*

"not
a Faberge egg
that you keep
        forever
pass down

to heirs"

*

"a box of candy
(a gift
    you eat
        then pass
around)"

*

"From the night
I met her
        I knew
she'd be mine
she begged
for

my collar
                    (much more
than a gift)"

             *

"A true slave
          would not
put limits
          on
the submission"

             *

"When one sits
          with a dying friend
          is that not
a gift of self?
          (submission too a gift
of self)"

             *

"I was born
          with a submissive
spirit
          that is my gift
(like a gift
          for music
or painting)"

             *

"How many times
        have we heard
the phrase
        a gift of kindness"

                *

"Trust is an act of faith,
                        not a gift"

                *

"I thought I was into
        sadonecrobondage
anddisciplineS&M
        but now I see
I am just flogging
        a dead horse"

                *

"A Domme friend
        told me a story
that she came home
        to find her
14 year-old flogging
        the dog
and the dog
loved it"

                *

"Like all relations,
        give and take,
take and give"

[inspired by the myth we summarized]

a non-human
woman
          births
taros & plants
animals
return to her
the source
(whose gift is free)

          indebted to the powers
no counter-gift
          can measure
                    we slaughter
a man
with bat-bone
needles in
          kidneys lungs neck
& head
                    cook the heart
make gardens
from his blood
          the cult-house
the richness
                    the bones
are used

in rituals
to grow

                to say
and to hide
                all social relations

we trick
                      ourselves
daily

into
our power

reality   measured
                by work
and death
until a suitable
contract
is made
between
man
& himself
                (who signs below)

[the return of the ring]

a fault-based
approach
ends in a break-up
(of rituals
and rites,
       their permutations)
did, for instance,
the parties
       have
       a hasty proposal
nothing
in common
          hated in-laws
a hostile child

disagreeable pets

          untidy habits
       a view of what
       went wrong
          in the promise
       makes us believe
          in fairness & truth
(though Roman law
says
       he gets

the ring—she
        a penalty
for reneging—)
the rule of life
        as rule of law
you break
it off
        you lose
the gift
unless she's
at fault
        (and leaving town)
which might mean
trickery
        and cover
    of night

(I picture Mae West

or a film
noir blonde
with sultry eyes
        and a cash
register mind)

        "give back the ring
get on with your life"
        is common sense

(minus
insult & rage)
both parties
        walk
away
from the scene
        like dancers
 who slump
            after the dance
yet
we hope
to learn
from things
        a lesson
transmuting
gold
        into grace

[one in space, the other in time]

I need opacity
        to see myself—
clearly—
        through prayers
                & sacrifice
as I exist
        it is my wish
        to make
                a world
through laws
        and then
to miss
                the recognition
amnesia
a fact
        of all between—

the what of things—
        the things
of man—
which stand in

        at the altarpiece

        defying time

& recognition
       a salt exchange
results in praise
       (and sometimes death
in higher doses)
       & semen too
a type of salt
       each gift the poison
of human position
       when my
duplications
   represent me
       in volition
& desire

[the walls are thine]

united as bride
   & groom
he receives
what
is ours
   & transfers
to us
   what is his
("a happy exchange")
gives us
   righteousness
takes over
our sins
     his death
atonement
   our righteousness
an imputation

("Is this the promised end?
Or image of that horror?")

   but here

(we object)

   credit
won't

transfer
from
      flesh
to spirit
(*"vex not his ghost:*
    oh let him pass")

      unless there
is "faith which
lays
      hold
and enfolds
      as the ring
      enfolds
the precious stone"
      so he
  appropriates
our guilt
      (said Luther)
yet

our sins do speak
      as water

or wind—
      & accidents
result

          Lear dies
before
our eyes
          in time
    no famous
words
("Ein alter Mann
          ist stets
ein König Lear")
          who gives it
                    all away
without receipt
          of love

[the heart, a dwelling-house]

these votive
offerings
these vows
to the
"sacrarium"
seat
"or organ
of love"
in order
to
make holy
we offer
"a victim"
who communicates
between
sacred
& profane
we destroy
by virtue
of ceremony

an object
by fire
(broken

or otherwise)

       wary of
"fetichism"
        "cardiolatry"
we transition
      to gifts
   breaking
from bloodshed
      and totem to
feast

     when
the heart
is right to

   rejoice
  without
     burning

[we live today in the world as it is]

to atone
for his earlier work
      (the slash between
breasts)
alone in the church
      of his verbal
description
he divorced
temporal

      from spiritual
        to say it simply
the photos changed
      as did the myth
        of reconciliation
      (in war too
      an immense consumption
      of men & goods)
behind the parts
an impossible freedom

      of cannon fire
   & altarpiece
seized by the agony
      in his photos

      we gave it a realm
    in which to grow
& in our generosity

                a countenance
of its own
                        ("priesthood a club
whose members are dead")
                to leave his mark
on culture
                as such
                        to form a bridge
from our lives
                to the thick
of contemplation
                (both dangerous and active)
rejecting the efforts
                of collaboration with
the information

                he worked alone
making small

                invisible bombs
                (to wrench himself free)
from fire
                        whose gift

was for burning
                                from acquisitiveness
whose particles
                were history

[to animate his work, prometheus]

vandalized the world
       fire & breath
stolen
       (in a dry season)

"the necessity of the crime"
       married foresight
to hope
       beginnings added later
           susceptible to hindsight
(we say it started
on *that* day
             or *this*)
casting a spell
       (angelic
          or monstrous)
all the same
our words
the gift
       feet set
    on earth

how cruel

a god   to let

              us warm
our hands
              and still to burn

we make
              a world
required of
incompleteness

                      in the image
              of imperfection
light learns
              its proper name

[a group's intended eternity is always at risk from depradation]

envy as

  the mainspring

    of demand
self-made rules

form a triangle
  "of honor

    luck &

      shame"
avenging gods

replaced by novelty

    "free floating desire"

        "voices overlap
and blend"
"shadows slip

    through shadows"

        future and past

          "allegory
a destination

    one can long for"

        "Golden was the first

        age   which

kept faith

    and did

the right"
               next world—
a bribe
      for losing
this—

all Hamlets
      with a gift
            for monologue

[the bare and empty sky of equivalences]

visibility itself
        (what the eye
can witness)
        daily in a mind
"grandly simple"
        evidence   (traces
of body fluid)
                discloses to us
the secret
        relationship
to nothing
(his nothing was mine/mine a nothing/that his could break)
        they took a photo
in the whale's belly
                that was they
now
        as in memory
implying redemption
        (redeem me/she said/to the nothing/around her)
the moment ousted   .
        was physical pain
his story
        of progress

        ("society's worst form
of cant")
        from here
to there

there was nothing
                to be done
        nothing to set right
the pretext of care
        location

of the narrative
            (from an obvious place
to another)
            he told it
                    emerging from shadows
his gift for telling
(the freedom
we call morals)
            about
the fact
of his intention
            (she lay in bed all day)

the psychic life   silent
        life of the heart

transposed
            to interior monologue
        her gift for telling
            not succor
or charity
            she kept it inside her—

"the mystique of saving"
      don't blame the author
for the story's waste
      don't blame that
which she loved
      for its reticence

Notes

PAGE 11: Lewis Hyde, *The Gift*

PAGE 12: Ralph Waldo Emerson, *Gifts*

PAGE 13: Marcel Mauss, *Gift, Gift*

PAGE 14: Emile Benviniste, *Gift and Exchange in the Indo-European Vocabulary*

PAGE 15: Claude Levi-Strauss, *Introduction to the Work of Marcel Mauss*

PAGE 16: Marshall Sahlins, *Stone-Age Economics*

PAGE 17: Rudolphe Gasche, *Heliocentric Exchange*

PAGE 18: Jacques Derrida, *The Time of the King*

PAGE 19: Various Walt Whitman poems

PAGE 20: Poems by Elizabeth Barrett Browning, William Shakespeare, Walt Whitman, Ted Berrigan, and John Donne

PAGE 21: Ansel Adams, letter to Cedric Hardwick

PAGES 22-23: Helene Cixous and Catherine Clement, *The Newly Formed Woman*

PAGES 24-25: Luce Irigaray, *Women on the Market*

PAGE 26: Rainer Maria Rilke, *The Duino Elegies*

PAGE 27: Pierre Bourdieu, *The Logic of Practice*

PAGE 28: Rainer Maria Rilke, *The Duino Elegies*

PAGE 29: Pierre Bourdieu, *Marginalia*

PAGE 30: Allan Stoekl, *Bataille, Gift-giving, and the Cold War*

PAGES 31-32: Robert Bernasconi, *What Goes Around Comes Around*

PAGES 33-34: Gary Shapiro, *The Metaphysics of Presents*

PAGE 35: Graham Greene, *The Quiet American*

PAGE 36: Definition of prayer, *Encyclopedia of Theology*

PAGES 37-38: Genevieve Vaughan, *A Feminist Critique of Exchange*

PAGES 39-42: www.dungeonrealm.com

PAGES 43-44: Maurice Godelier, *The Sacred*

PAGES 45-47: *The Question of the Ring,* www.divorcesource.com

PAGES 48-49: Maurice Godelier, *Substitute Objects for Humans and Gods*

PAGES 50-52: *Theology Today: Atonement and Saving Faith*

PAGES 53-54: Definition of sacrifice, *International Standard Bible Encyclopedia*

PAGES 55-56: John Berger, *About Looking,* John-Paul Sartre, *What Is Literature?*

PAGES 57-58: Peter Conrad, *The Foresight of Prometheus*

PAGES 59-60: Mary Douglas and Baron Isherwood, *The World of Goods,* Grant McCracken, *Culture and Consumption,* Peter Conrad, *Opera and Literary Form*

PAGES 61-63: John Berger, *About Looking,* John-Paul Sartre, *What Is Literature?*

PHOTO: Paul Hoover

MAXINE CHERNOFF is the author of six collections of fiction, including the *New York Times Book Review* Notable Book of 1993, *Signs of Devotion*. Both her novel, *American Heaven*, and her book of short stories, *Some of Her Friends that Year*, were finalists for the Bay Area Book Reviewers Award. Her seven books of poetry include *World: Poems 1991-2001* and *Evolution of the Bridge: Selected Prose Poems* (Salt Publishing, Cambridge, England). Editor of *New American Writing*, she lives with poet Paul Hoover and their three children in Mill Valley, California.